VANISHMENTS

Also by Eric Pankey

The History of the Siege (2024)
Not Yet Transfigured (2021)
Alias (2020)
Vestiges: Notes, Responses & Essays (2019)
Owl of Minerva (2019)
Augury (2017)
Crow-Work (2015)
Dismantling the Angel (2014)
Trace (2013)
The Pear as One Example: New and Selected Poems (2008)
Reliquaries (2005)
Oracle Figures (2003)
Cenotaph (2000)
The Late Romances (1997)
Apocrypha (1991)
Heartwood (1988)
For the New Year (1984)

VANISHMENTS

poems

ERIC PANKEY

SL/NT
BOOKS

VANISHMENTS
Poems

Copyright © 2025 Eric Pankey. All rights reserved. Except for brief quotations in critical publications or reviews, no part of this book may be reproduced in any manner without prior written permission from the publisher. Write: Permissions, Slant Books, P.O. Box 60295, Seattle, WA 98160.

Slant Books
P.O. Box 60295
Seattle, WA 98160

www.slantbooks.org

Cataloguing-in-Publication data:

Names: Pankey, Eric.

Title: Vanishments: poems / Eric Pankey.

Description: Seattle, WA: Slant Books, 2025

Identifiers: ISBN 978-1-63982-197-6 (hardcover) | ISBN 978-1-63982-196-9 (paperback) | ISBN 978-1-63982-198-3 (ebook)

Subjects: LCSH: Poetry | American poetry | American poetry 21st century

For Jennifer on our fortieth anniversary

In my room, the world is beyond my understanding;
But when I walk I see that it consists of three or four hills and a cloud.

—*Wallace Stevens*

Contents

Precisely What We See | 1

I

Lost While Looking for a Glacial Lake | 5
Confluence | 6
Field Recording | 9
Land Parcels Stitched Together | 10
Desire Path | 11
Evening Estuary | 14
Divination of Hidden Things *[The Hazel]* | 15
The Past | 16
Margins | 17
Sonatina for Donald Justice | 18

II

Sonatina for Mark Strand | 21
Knucklebone Oracle | 22
Jackstraws | 25
Draft of a Landscape | 27
Misty Fjords | 28
Held Up to a Flame the Writing Is Visible | 29
The Edge | 30
Variations on a Theme by Leopardi | 31
Inner Passage | 32
Variations on a Theme by Ponge | 33

III

The Ruin | 37
Requiem | 38
Verifying the Atrocities | 39
Evening Commotion | 40
Offstage Shipwreck | 41
Vanishments | 42
A Minor Treatise on Tenebrism | 43
House with Many Rooms | 44
True Knowledge | 45
Negative Spaces | 46

IV

The House of the Muse | 53
Raveled Threads | 54
Notes Home | 55
The Initiate | 56
In the Midst of Omens | 57
Displacement | 58
The Binding | 59
The Epic | 60
Dwelling Place | 61
Empty Calendar | 62

V

Empty Space with Radio Waves | 69
Lilith's Dream | 70
Afterbodings | 71
Stone City | 75
To Paint the Circumference of a Stone with a Feather | 76
Relocation | 81
Sacred Spaces | 82
With Hidden Noise | 83
Drought | 84
Departures | 85

Acknowledgments | 87
Notes | 89

PRECISELY WHAT WE SEE

Not the thing, but the perfect rhyming
Of its name: *chestnut husk.*

The indexical impulse, of course,
Calls attention to all that's left out,
Not yet indexed, named, listed, enumerated
Or included as an item in the inventory.

One adds a stone to the cairn
But does not know what element
Will dislodge it, send it tumbling.

Nothing is more difficult,
Maurice Merleau-Ponty writes
In *The Phenomenology of Perception,*
Than to know precisely what we see.

Hard not to envy the mirror's detachment.

Although the bed is empty, it is still called a *river.*

I

LOST WHILE LOOKING FOR A GLACIAL LAKE

High in the mountain: frostbitten light.
Late May. Dwarf alpine daffodils.

Weather-pocked rocks.
                              Half-way down:
A waterfall widened into a stream. Steppingstones

Swept haphazardly across a shallow bend.
Crag martins dash and loop.

Hot sun. Chill air.
                       Even then the words
Were out of reach: a cold depth I could not fathom.

CONFLUENCE

Two crows return; take
                        a look at the overlooked;
Caw out their findings.

        ::

Not the *edge*,
            but *approaching-the-edge*.
The horizon: a thicket of static.

        ::

The extraneous is stripped away,
                          nonetheless pollen
Velvets each surface.

        ::

At the confluence: slippages,
                          crosscurrents,
An eddy outside the drift.

        ::

Eden, snatched away
                by eminent domain,
Hovers in the distant heat haze as mirage.

                ::

As we have come to know,
                the *unsaid* gets infected,
Manifests itself as an inwrought burl of silence.

                ::

An eddy outside the drift—
                an oracular glyph
Eludes, as always, legibility.

                ::

When I put in green,
                Matisse would say, *it is not grass.*
When I put in blue, it is not the sky.

                ::

The bees retrace
                a crazed path among the yarrow.
Refraction and reflection interweave the water's weft.

::

With higher magnification,
                    we can inspect
The seemingly simple form's complexity.

::

Landscape, the scale
                on which time is measured,
Leans at day's end toward darkness.

::

Change *is* constant—
                    form gives way to form:
An eddy outside the drift.

FIELD RECORDING

A mortarless stone wall follows the hill, then tumbles.

Where a path threads deep shade, a hazel
Oversees the cold lap and gabble of a holy well;
A door, relieved of its function, serves as a table

(*An arrangement*, as in music;
                            an adaptation,

A working with, or through, what already exists.)
The semblance is fixed, yet memory weathers
In unforeseen ways: the accord, the calm

Of three notes sounded at once: *water, hazel, stone.*

LAND PARCELS STITCHED TOGETHER

The snow buffers the sound of its own
Accumulation. The sky intrudes.
Without collision, galaxies cross.
The end deferred for now. Postponed.
The moments, shaved back to whispers,
Are held fast as the ice crystals set:
Each anonymous and singular.

: :

It takes so little to fill an empty mind.
Clouds crowd then part. The sky clears.
The island is an amalgam of weathers,
Land parcels stitched together
With stone walls. Misty intervals
At dusk and dawn. Whale bones
Like a shattered raft on the beach.

DESIRE PATH

Among a wall's tumbled stones,
The broken hinge of a sheep's jaw.

::

A bog pool holds the sky:
Cloud-strewn. Murky. Gray.

::

A worn path as evidence of concurrence.
Drying nets as a temporary fence.

::

The past is brooding turbulence.
The future: the flat horizon's allure.

::

The hillside heather-clad;
An island socked in with fog.

::

An undersong of wind through grasses:
The strata of hours accrue slowly.

::

Hollow limestone underfoot.
Calcium grit where puddles evaporate.

::

Rusty black-fern thrive here
As well as bloody crane's-bill.

::

Dwarf blackthorn.
Honeysuckle and holly.

::

From overturned sand, midges lift.
At low tide the shell heap stinks.

::

A snarl of fishing line snagged
In the thatch. A ligature of gull mewls.

::

An archive of touch, a ledger of looks,
A chart of all the dead stars.

::

Neither the starting point nor
The destination is fixed or known.

::

Fissured limestone: glacier rasped,
Scoured clean. Clints and grykes.

::

Spray. Mists. Droplets. Rain.
A window frames the exterior.

EVENING ESTUARY

Is there a view from the path?
Or is it
     a view from the past?
What surmounts the gap after *the after?*

No answers in the stars.
Zero holds its place.
                       Signifies nothing.
Widening into the wetland:

The salt creek, the *now* of thunder.
Sediments—
              emergent strata—
Shift and settle and are buried.

DIVINATION OF HIDDEN THINGS [THE HAZEL]

        Hermes braids a staff of hazel wood

           fire springs from a hazel branch

               lichen on the hazel's grayish-brown bark

                    hazel catkins in cold wind

nightjars and willow warblers alight in a coppiced hazel

                      I cut hazel rods for dowsing

      at the midpoint of the Otherworld, a hazel

    magnesium, potassium, and copper enrich the hazel nut

       for a thatching spar, slit a hazel gad

         below the hill of Tara, a hazel festooned with votive offerings

             four woven hazel-wattle hurdles enclose a sacred space

               hazel understory beneath birch and oak

         into a holy well, a hazel drops plump late autumn fruit

           while harvesting hazel wands on Sunday, I meet the Devil

THE PAST

It's an imprecise aggregation, forgotten as it is documented:
A prism of sorts, a magnetic field, a pentimento of reflections. The data,
Contingent, will certainly be adjusted. Or mothballed. Like a hundred
    photographs
Taken of different bodies of water at different hours, and then displayed
With the horizons aligned, it's nowhere really.
                                       Talons entangled, two hawks
Cartwheel and plummet, accelerate to terminal velocity: a thorny snarl of
    loose ends,
A skirmish of scribbles, an isolated event, all nuance, or the lack thereof.

MARGINS

I stare but seeing does not deepen.
A gaze is absorbed. A gaze is reflected.

::

Clouds gather. A bramble of thunder.
A serpent cannot be coaxed to swallow its own tail.

::

Each thought set down like alluvium.
As *periphery* is to *blind spot*. . .

::

The solvent allows the image to transfer
From this surface to that: reversed, ghostly.

::

The day's margins lose their edge:
Solidity sublimes into vapor.

SONATINA FOR DONALD JUSTICE

Drops on a rain-chain.
One tone, then another.

The gray octave dampened,
Rubbed out. What remains?

The silent repetition of silence.
Ghost notes. A score of rest.

II

SONATINA FOR MARK STRAND

One arrives from the future to disrupt an event in the past. A side effect of time travel is that one arrives in the past with no memory of the future. Now, in the past, unaware of one's task, one watches, powerless to intervene, the event occur as it must.

One arrives from the future to find that loops and skeins of roots entwine the reclining Buddha. There is a pause in the monsoon. Clouds are mended and re-torn. Having arrived from the future, one is hungry, naked, and of slender means.

One arrives from the future as if from a shoreless ocean, a darkened room, a circle formed by standing stones not original to the site.

One arrives from the future, uninvited, as welcome as a beggar, as unnoticed. The past is always there—there in the distance—a thinning cloud of squid ink.

KNUCKLEBONE ORACLE

How to reconcile chance
And randomness when each
Gives way predictably to disorder?

∷

The dust rubbed away
Incises and mars the glass.

∷

Is Mars in retrograde?
                No—
That's a withered rosehip,
A clot, a scabby clinker.

∷

A dusk-moon's dull luster;

The speed and trajectory
Of a barn owl's plummet.

∷

Things accumulate by way of negation;
Change via intervention.

           ::

Like the interrogation room's
Two-way mirror, an oracle
Reveals and conceals.

           ::

Shadows contradict their hour.
From the undifferentiated, questions arise.

           ::

The ocean resists description.
Air and depth. Surface and salt.
Each movement: unforeseen.

           ::

A dream is available in its moment.
After that it is a species of dust.

::

The architecture of the past

(An arabesque of tendrils and leaves,
Fragile bones carved from chalk)

Is lit by an absent source of light.

::

The future shivers and shimmers
With the not-quite-perfect
Stillness of a *tableau vivant*.

::

And now?
A window open to rain.

JACKSTRAWS

In preparation for the wolf, a sharpened ax is placed hearthside.

A ship, overwhelmed by storm waves, founders in Act One, Scene One.

The intelligence gleaned from radio chatter confirms the *already known*.

Discord is introduced into the *tableau vivant* as a wounded antelope.

Dark and without depth: a vacant theater set, a display window, a diorama.

In the corner, a spider, attuned to the irrational, knits a length of sleep.

A wick smokes, unspools the acrid odor of burnt dust, of a star snuffed out.

Unruly threads and fibers—plucked at, pulled loose—disrupt the weave's grid.

A ghost is but a moment—elongated, smeared—erasure that does not rid but distorts.

Plankton adrift. The farthest star remains to be seen. A word weighs less than a wit.

The moon is hung impossibly low in the sky: an ache, a bone set to mend.

In the adagio of a metronome, even stillness flees: a needle alert to the idea of *North*.

Being and non-being give birth to one another: a skein of lace, a box of buttons.

The awaited-upon moment has occurred already repeatedly.

The canyon wall's striations, wrought by water, by wind, reveal deviation in the parallel of lines.

A pond becomes meadow, a meadow a pond over years. The present is unprecedented.

In the presence of a hawk, songbirds quiet. Time, a sickle blade, circles back on itself.

An upset bucket? A folding chair? How few objects make of a stage a bridal chamber? A ruined temple?

Clear cold air magnifies moss filaments, pine pollen, the gray varve of glacial sediment.

No sound of an ax. Rivers and mountains emerge from mist. Re-vanish.

DRAFT OF A LANDSCAPE

After Paul Celan

Crow-wings blue in noon-light.

The poppy petal flesh-like—
No—papery.
              Bird-clatter
In a hollow, strung-up calabash.

A towpath by the river. Tidemarks
Imprinted on memory.
                       Cloud's
Windward edge ragged and frayed.

Hornets—a host of fallen angels—
Amass above the winepress.
                         Barbs strewn
Irregularly along the wire.

A window makes the world
A rectangle,
            makes distance
A script that refuses legibility.

Noon-light bluing the crow's black.

MISTY FJORDS

Degrees of impermanence

Transient clouds scud above

Slow geologic movement

Steep cliffs jut up from water

Recorded at intervals

Time becomes the subject

Bivouacked as we are

In the present tense

The current would have us elsewhere

HELD UP TO A FLAME THE WRITING IS VISIBLE

Removed as I am by language

From immediacy, the narrative
Retains somehow the precarious
Illusion of time passing. Innumerable

Vanishing points, like a saint's wounds,
Pierce the surface. What is the atomic weight
Of *melancholy*? Where in the hierarchy

Of sorrows does one place a *dead mother*
Or a *lost love belatedly appreciated*?
The past is there—dense, weighty, sunken—

An anchor around which the present pivots.

THE EDGE

At water's edge, the old growth forest
Doubles reflected in fjord-depths.

The waterfall, quick in the path it carved,

Switchbacks. Roots overlap, intertwine.
The understory confined to shadows.

Sedges give way to boggy meadow.

Dew glints on lichens and spiders' webs.
Tonight, a mist-dimmed moon will light the way

To what we have passed and what is to come.

It's easier to imagine the infinite a little
Larger than to subtract from a sum

Not yet reached. Rock. Sea. Sky.

VARIATIONS ON A THEME BY LEOPARDI

From the Zodiac boat, he looked back and saw the ship,
Miniature beneath the U-shaped valley rising as granite above it,

The clouds like something out of a Chinese ink drawing.
Serpentine. More dragons than insubstantial mist or vapor.

Why was he looking back when they had traveled the rough distance
To feel cold wind off the glacier's face, to watch as it advanced and calved,

To hear a crack echo against the unnamed range, to bob in the wake of the sudden fall?
As in a dream, he found himself *in between*, unable to arrive or depart—

Too early or, more likely, belated, delayed, encumbered, overdue—
Foundered and adrift, without a sextant to gauge the infinite.

INNER PASSAGE

Moss and sedges. Alders intrude.

A rucksack of dream heavy with glacial silt.
The blunt blade-edge of a story whetted.

Hemlock and spruce lag. Day-moon:

A pecked-at, washed-up bone.
The harbor seal's head emerges:

A glint. Eyes open, it submerges.

Archipelago of old growth rainforest.
Root-wads and slash snagged on sandbars.

An iceberg topples; shows its underside:

Blue against water's opaque celadon.
Cold slurry of glacial flour.

Bunchberry on the inner forest floor.

Toppled, lichen-scuffed: a totem pole's
Third life as a nurse log.

VARIATIONS ON A THEME BY PONGE

When a wildfire at last
Collapses, spent,

One considers the quiet
Modesty of stones,

How the present
Is at once ephemeral

And persistent.
After a poem,

What is left?
Words defined

In reference
To other words.

III

THE RUIN

It's like some tool the function of which
Is forgotten.
            Or a caribou antler
Worn by fast-moving sediment.

Or like a form present in itself, an alloy of spirit
And substance, say,
                    or like lines I must move
To expand the space between them.

Or like that calligraphic gesture at bluff's edge—
Inked in between fog
                  and sunlight's
Unsayable imperative—the aimless gesture

I call *a wind-bent tree.*

REQUIEM

After the battle:
>a fallen feather
With which to fletch a damaged arrow.

The vastness is nondescript,
Anonymous:
>a half-formed thought.

To the east:
>willows green.
A dragonfly alights on a dewdrop.

Ravens and wind fashion a fugue.

VERIFYING THE ATROCITIES

Lightning lights everything all at once.
It is only afterward that one recalls the *seen*.

∷

The benefits of hindsight.
The narcotic effect of the hour.

∷

As the backhoe uncovers the mass grave,
the bones of the dead mingle.

∷

Rain ceases. Wiper blades scrape.
One needs to find a room for the night.

∷

Each thought interrupted by the next,
By what one calls *thinking*.

EVENING COMMOTION

A skirr of bats. A stitch of swallows.
The day is scuttled in depths of dark.
A lance of moonlight bisects the scene.

Two ladders are brought to bear
And the battered body, slinked in riggings
Of rope and cloth, shimmied down,

Its balance tipping this way and that.
Such weeping. The hurly-burly of grief.

OFFSTAGE SHIPWRECK

Beneath the willow's veiled green world,
The taut moon is a strung bow.

Low light casts splayed shadows.
An owl hunts over a sloping field.

A petite creek (or is it a large snake?)
Slips between thin scrub to intertidal sedges.

A breaking wave lifts, nudges
The exhausted castaways awake:

Battered. Waterlogged. Weak.
Their thirst, unslaked, burns as salt burns.

VANISHMENTS

Fog. No wind.
           Vapor
An apparition of itself.

The *seen* disappears.
Then takes form:

The phenomenology
Of the mutable.

Where ink adheres:
A willow,
        perhaps,

Translucent
          beyond—
Smeared, occluded.

A façade of logic,
Haze brings distance close.

A MINOR TREATISE ON TENEBRISM

        The crowberry's blackish
Cobalt is neither
            Obsidian nor basalt.

        It reflects a fleck
Or, perhaps, a flash
            As an opal might,

        Of skimmed-milk white
On the taut curve
            Of the fruit's dark

            And darkening ripe.

HOUSE WITH MANY ROOMS

I recollect the depths of shadow,
The uncertain elsewhere of each room,
Dust like stellar remnants drawn together.
As I cross a threshold, the room
Departed vanishes as if a stage set
On which the lights have been cut.
I have no choice but to move ahead,
And cannot help but feel an interloper,
Guilty of some voyeuristic intrusion,
Although the rooms are empty, unoccupied.
Perhaps ahead a furnished room waits:
A thin veneer of moonlight on a quilt.
Black crepe draped over the mirror.

TRUE KNOWLEDGE

The past lingers in the body like lead.

Far from the city, a deep quarry from which each stone
That built the city was excavated and carried.

A snake basks on slate. No one could foretell

The series of premonitions that followed, or
The warm clarity of a Provençal sky: minimal shadow,

Pines resinous in wind and heat.

I always have a good reason for taking something out,
Robert Rauschenberg says, *but never have one for putting something in.*

Ferrous oxide as pigment; horse grease as medium.

Two birds harry a fox. True knowledge hovers
Like a flame above the enlightened one's head.

NEGATIVE SPACES

A little breath.
     A fox slowed by deep snow.
A poem begins as it ends.

Deer have carved a little basin atop the salt lick.
There snow melts, pools. Lifts again as vapor.

A circle of flint stones. A slurry of icy river mud.
The sky is not blue, but blues recur.

A poem ends as it begins.
       A little breath.
A fox slowed by deep snow.

    ::

Contained in a body,
     I imagine transcendence.
Doubt is never singular but gathers like a swarm.
Suppose my various atoms occupy limitless space

And never touch.
     And never do not touch. Which
Then is an intimacy and which an intrusion? Winter

Light, pulled thin, withdraws, leaves the past intact.
I retrace my own itinerancy, curate this body as an archive.

    ::

The stream carries the mountain away
                              grain by grain,
The stream that carved the cliff-edge.

The emptiness,
           restless, gives into becoming.
I have descended halfway down the mountain

To dwell among clouds.
                     In the stream depth:

A trout's departure—a quick flint-spark.

Clarity ripples,
             roughed with glacial silt.

Before a single iota has coalesced from the murk
Of *not-yet-ness*,
              I am lost in thought.

                   : :

At wood's edge, buttercups and violets.

A sycamore split head-high by lightning.
A shallow pit ringed with skunk cabbage.

Through the April gloom,
                     a white gash of dogwood bracts.

I am not surprised by this fleeting feeling I call the *spiritual*,

Nor by the rupture of an interruption. Scent lingers
Like time lingers. Then dissipates.

                   : :

Behind whatever house I've lived in,
A slow creek shimmers in leaf-light.
Roots dangle along the undercut bank.
Some days: the aimless skitter of rain.
Some days: clouds emerge from slow depths.

As I sweep up the thread-ends of thoughts,
The path steepens into dusk
As if departure could leave no trace.
Who knows what startles the crows?
A clatter of leaves swirls up.

::

All fog and gull-cry. The undertow tugs seaward.
The skiff unmoored. Adrift.
                        Its tether worn away:
A dragged, useless wick. On shore, the bonfire sputters.
Flinders ascend above flames, stand in for stars.

I am, as always, under the weather and leave
Behind a narrative of missteps,
                        of involuntary traces.
Fog hangs: a worn gray drop cloth, a noiseless waterfall.
A wreck of detritus delineates the high tide mark.

With an old gospel song snagged in my head—
A remote echo
           that fades and swells,
Expands and collapses over its duration—
I attempt and fail again at *not knowing*.

::

Sky balanced upon a flooded meadow.
A brood of mists. A shapeshifter moon.

Water recalls the shape it filled.
The negative form: a vessel of sorts.

I wake to misplaced time,
The last shimmer of a din come to its end.

The vocabulary is simple,
The grammar untranslatable.

Of what use is the snake's shed skin
Or the part of prayer that is wordless?

I am off topic—entangled and engulfed—
Stuck here at the point of entry.

Time grows diffuse at the horizon—
A scumble of resists and erasures.

Dark matter overlooked.
I pry. I eavesdrop upon degrees

Of uncertainty, of secrecy.
Upon each word vying for attention.

::

The way back is just as long, scree loose underfoot, the weather worse—

Virga, like threads untucked from a hem, gives way to rainfall—
The landscape in grayscale.
                        I say the darkness descends, yet look
How it lifts right out of the ground like mist or fog. To mend it,
I must pierce the fabric, tug the frayed edges back together.

At least each stitch holds for now. How is setting out different
From returning, when both are shorn by forgetting of their pain?
Given cloud-cover: no stars, no moon.
                                    The landscape in grayscale:
Washed-out gradations, a dulled spectrum from *dovetail* to *pewter*.

       ::

I can only see down to a certain level
Through water's depth.
                    The transparencies stacked
Are opaque. I am never in the world not a body,

Not this single gesture repeated without meaning.
The horizon is a taut snap line,
                        a vibration
In the interstitial spaces of the seemingly solid.

To render the void, I cast the negative spaces:
Empty field. Open sky.
                    Wind at a threshold,
Suspended there, there in the meanwhile.

IV

THE HOUSE OF THE MUSE

With painstaking advances,
A snail revisits the earth
On a bent grass blade.

The path up the hill to the village

Is as thin as a whisper,
As rugged as a twisted rope.

Disturbed by roots: stony ground.

A ruined wall links two realms:
Cherry orchard and vineyard—
Cicada-abraded, swallow-skimmed.

Is *light* or *dark* the edge that divides?

RAVELED THREADS

Rain. Sleet.
           The river bears it away.

Beneath a pine, a bed of needles.
Between a crow's calls, snow slips to sleet.

The river darkens.
                  As if reciting

The same verse from the same sutra,
Another crow calls.

NOTES HOME

Ice on the pines.
                Cold

Realm of geometry:

Stark verticals against
A shadow-anchored mountain.

                     ::

A moment dilates,
                takes on mass.

Fog lags as tangled dark matter.

Rocky edges, tide pools,
Vast mudflats concealed.

                     ::

Moonlight.
          Or is it frost?

Low clouds hold down cliffs.

As if an afterthought:
The unamendable world.

THE INITIATE

Like a snake quick across a rain-wet

Path, I attempt to be nonchalant
In my disregard. After a series of false

Starts, I braid a rope of sisal, smoke,
And horsehair to index the passing of time.

I invent a grid of columns and rows

To pinpoint coordinates, an arrow to stand
In for the wind. I sing a sacred hymn

To Hypnos, the brother of Death,
And wait for the intervention of a reply,

The imposition of what happens next.

IN THE MIDST OF OMENS

                I have a fever,
Am an apparition, not a haunting,
A delirium of air, water, and fire.

I lack the faculty we call *a soul*.
Am some Adam extracted from a clay bank.
The path I make meanders like a river,

Finds the way that resists least. The water
Is ruddled. It drains away. Silts in.
An ocher wash. Like a rose, I am slumped,

Fragrance-heavy. A dead moth, I am
More weightless than a live one.
Illness makes me a stranger to myself,

Fraught, flummoxed. A minuet
On *replay* to accompany the deep time.
I am as willing as ever to accept the Gospel,

To be straw, rust, and charcoal,
To be the fury of a wetted axe-head
Making its way through wilderness.

DISPLACEMENT

Full or emptied of souls,
Charon's boat displaces
The same volume of water.

The towers are placed at intervals
Of no more than a bowshot apart.
Winds quarrel in the canopy.

In 1658, Thomas Browne writes,
But who knows the fate of his bones
Or how often he is to be buried?

As an old hymn gets broken down to blues,
There is this choice of honey or venom.

THE BINDING

Melted permafrost undermines

The level of a distant early warning
Radar station.
           A chalked snap line,
Submerged in rising waters, blurs.

A threaded darning needle,
Unused, rusts.
           A thicket's thorns pierce
A snagged ram's flesh as it struggles.

An angel stays a father's hand.

THE EPIC

What, in the end, is left:

Enough bones scattered
In the fields to build a city?

Enough bones scattered
In the fields to fashion
A ladder to the moon?

What set the epic in motion
In the first place? A grain of salt?

Salt distilled, perhaps,
From a single tear? A bit
Of grit around which pearled

Ten thousand lines of verse?

DWELLING PLACE

Of course, an empty space invites trespass.
A lock forced. A door thrown wide open
Sets the accumulated dust in motion.
No body is shaped from that dust,
No breath enkindles a specter,

Despite evidence to the contrary.
Moonlit motes illuminate the fallow space.
The interior, breached, remains entangled
In the past, but the trespasser finds it empty,
Which is to say: unsettled, disenchanted.

EMPTY CALENDAR

Snail-scrawl in tidal mud.
The drift of clouds as a compass.

A network of repetitions,
The chance encounter is prepared for.
Pale, luminous—a vast distance.

::

The moment comes around
At last: a votive offering,
A spill of house lights on the flooded marsh.

As I align the past with the present,
The foreground presses close.

::

The usual intervention of weather.
Shadows skew against the hour.

Faint fragments, as if web silk, aloft:
Ghostly, without weight. I
Renegotiate the diaphanous tangle.

::

With only a wooden match
As a unit of measure, I build a scale model.
Night, like an underpainting, bleeds through.

I proceed as if a title might
Allow at last the amalgam to set.

::

The *always* of a remembered detail.
The uneven terrain not yet worn even.

Not the stones, driftwood, or shell heap,
But the air, the breathable salt air, through which
I observe each as it levitates.

::

X equals the unknown, which is to say
The cussed, the otherwise irretrievable,
A negative space of clouds and mist.

What is memory but remote access?
Out of fog a depth of fog coalesces.

::

The event occurs, occurred, will occur
In a tense form available only in dream.

An island endures in the distance,
A beach of disheveled cobbles, as blue
As an anomaly of fire, as glacial melt.

∷

The poem is not a representation,
But an analogous experience.
Is it a hoax if no one is deceived?

This is yet another iteration,
A patina of marks and smears.

∷

I had hoped for a fragile transience,
For the ordinary's semblance of mystery.

What is a genre if not an interrogation
Of genre? How do I discern presence
When I reside in past light and lost time?

∷

The sky is without depth or surface.
No need to graph a range of nuances
As the tide pulls back, and the past flattens.

One season lapses into the next,
Into some uncharted calm or calamity.

::

The longing is not for a paradise, but
For its eventual, inevitable loss.

On a current's bewildered grammar
Fractured ice sheets refreeze. Cloud-like,
Distant lands recede as I draw near.

::

For more than a second, a ghost adheres
To sight, like a breath's aftereffect on glass:
No more bereft of meaning when it's gone.

I shelter in place. Day by day by day
I invent a place in which to shelter.

V

EMPTY SPACE WITH RADIO WAVES

Withered thistles hide the dropped scythe's
Rusted cutting-edge. In the aftermath,
How surprisingly orderly the previous order:
A staged tableau of error and effort,
A bone-certain and abstract utility.
The distant hills edge toward violet:
The rubbed velvet of a violin case.
Spores float on the pond's surface.
As consolation, randomness increases.

LILITH'S DREAM

       The dream, a serpent coiled in upon itself,
Seems barely there, hardly a threat,
              But a serpent nonetheless,

       With its clever way with words,
The *shush, shush, shush* as its belly winds around a tree
              And it stands at last on its hind legs as tall as the woman

       To whisper something into her ear,
To calm her, to reassure her, confirming
              What she has thought all along,

       That there is something amiss,
Something not right with this picture,
              That she is without antecedent, wholly new

       And thus, to the man monstrous:
A creature with vipers for hair,
              A beast to veil, to cover up, to conceal

       As one conceals a bit of leavening in a ball of dough,
Yet it grows unbidden; takes on a life
              Of its own; swells.

AFTERBODINGS

1. *Too Soon for Thunder*

You detach from pain.
                          Best to leave
The peacock feather where it fell.

You turn your back on the sun only
To face a long black shadow stretched out
Like some poor soul's flayed skin.

Better to inhabit than to interpret
The world.
           A chill at twilight.
The silence of a wren come to rest.

2. *Bound on the West by Land*

The sky, weightless, grays and thins.

A static vista. No wind. No birds.

Strung up by rigging, the horizon
Is a drawn-out tensile shore.

The charted tundra fades, fragments.

The irrational cousin of ice, water
Pools: without reflection—dark, milky.

Thaw collapses distant structures.

3. *Nests of Lightning*

Having been cast ashore by shipwreck,
With only birch pitch for glue, with memory
Still pending, you consider first water, then shelter.

(The weather here does not allow
For the luminous blue of lapis lazuli.)

You approach the island's forest ax-handle-first,
Say, *I am one of you. You have nothing to fear.*
The blade-wedge heavy in your palms.

4. *At the Appointed Time*

The jackstraw observatory—a scaffold of smooth,

Salt-bleached driftwood—teeters in the least wind.
The past is not quite dormant, not quite latent:
A crisscross of microscopic cells. A directionless space.

With a thousand wormholes as ocular openings,
A small army of watchers can watch, though not one
Is awake. Shifts in sleep stagger time's cadence.

Is that a pileated woodpecker? Or its echo?

5. *Arithmetic of the Wind*

After sounding the depths
Your mind seldom clears.
$$1+1+1=$$

The unresolved narrative,
The shock of paradox.
                         You set off

With an outdated map of the arctic.
Fire, though not hungry,
                         feeds, moves

With a broom's knowledge of edges
Across the arid present,
                         the verdant past.

6. *Suspension Bridge for the Swallows*

As exhausted as a keener at a wake,

How to graft a gaze onto the *seen*
And still claim to be a bystander,
Innocent, or otherwise?

                         Overhead,
A coterie of swallows swirls up
Into a vortex and collapses: a sail

Denied its function. The moment
Is fixed like a single vanishing point.

7. *Journal of the Conjuror*

A dome of city lights bleaches out evening.
                                        Beneath
Poured concrete, a grid of rusted rebar. Some bones.

You scroll down for English,
                        sift through silence.
Consider the contested territory, the acceptable risk.

The spectrum's narrow range spans
                                grays and ochres.
Does the hyphen conjoin or keep separate *this* and *that*?

It could be any Wednesday.
                        Tomorrow, for example,
A motion that has not yet, but will perhaps, cease.

8. *The Secret Journey of a Spark*

You reinscribe the foreboding,
But more neatly, in a legible hand.
The idiom is entirely abstract,
Like the constraint of time upon a still image,

Like a fog-displaced mountain.
Decay already implicit. Ruin as reminder.
No, everything in the end is not *fine*.
In the end, everything is *fire*.

STONE CITY

Where *here* and *there* rub up,
A horizon. A torsion. A tension.

Hints of burnt umber amid greens.

The totality of time embodied
As a minor miracle, as depth of field:

A spent limestone quarry, a wide bend

Of deciduous trees along the Wapsipinicon,
The Quaker quiet of a meeting house.

TO PAINT THE CIRCUMFERENCE OF A STONE WITH A FEATHER

To proceed, one mars the surface.
One braids a rope of tattered prayer flags.

::

A whisper heightens attention.
A breeze animates a mirage.

::

Gust-shimmered, distorted: the intimate
Proximity of one's own reflection.

::

Nothing happens by chance, but by
An algorithm that simulates chance.

::

Turning against the current,
A slow whirlpool below the falls.

::

The gray amasses. Cold sea mist.
The island is crowned in rain.

::

What does one call the world
Under the underworld?

::

Umbra, penumbra, antumbra.
Almost forgotten, the past lurks.

::

A toxic cloud. A fatal error.
A repository of static. A trap and refuge.

::

Is memory time distilled
Or is it time diluted?

::

One digs in sand. Sand encroaches.
The angle of projection distorts an image.

::

As an offering to Pan, a canker
Grows in the shadow of abundance.

::

To postpone the pastoral's obsolescence,
One reconstructs a prairie from memory.

::

Insubstantial hills against haze:
A body. A surface projected onto.

::

Empty haywain. A thaw at midwinter.
To document the ephemeral, one looks away.

::

One has next to nothing.
One has a needle to repair the damage.

::

A grit of erasure nubs
Brushed aside to *the-verge-of.*

::

One detects erratic interference,
A subtle shift in signal.

::

A constellation of fireflies
Inside the camera obscura.

::

To disrupt the notion
Of permanence: a throw of the dice.

::

Where the parallel converges,
Drifting snow obliterates tracks.

::

A fragile light a billion years old;
A speck of dust to tip the equilibrium.

::

Shadows fold into night. Thread
Spun from milk connects constellations.

::

Underfoot: an entanglement of mycelium.
Just how low is *under the radar*?

::

The space between is as noteworthy,
One might argue, as the lines themselves.

RELOCATION

Smoke lifts from sinkholes, hovers. Or is it suspended?
An acute drabness makes of the place a backdrop,
Not a vista. Depth defies perspectival logic.
Down empty train tracks, I take measure of uncertainty,
Trespass in an exclusion zone,
                              balance on a rail,
Teeter at a tipping point. How to right myself
On a fault line that is the place of memory?
The coal seam has burned now for fifty years.
What is a ghost town ghosts have abandoned?

SACRED SPACES

The image blurs where a solvent spilled.

A veil of language lifts away
Like a basket of birds thrown in the air.
An arbitrary trace of the past remains:

Snow through a broken skylight.
Snow erasing the paths deer inscribe.
Snow terse and somber on the river

Where red vanishes from the visible spectrum.

WITH HIDDEN NOISE

I lack, I fear, the memoirist's essential tool—

Memory. Narrative as well is elusive:
A long exposure of ambient lights,
Smudged contours, overlapping spaces,

Barely recollected dreams stitched together
With milkweed silk. I return to the observable
World for more observation, but find

A calibrated space, neither cramped nor expansive;
Find the present moment at the periphery;
Find the veils and skeins of the auroras;

Find a rope with which to raise the scenery.
A myth grows up around me like a coppice.
Like a cage. The ball of twine (salvaged

From a maze's dead end) is held between
Two metal plates with screws. Within
The ball something is hidden and rattles.

A diamond? A coin? A dime-store trinket?
Without the presence of gravity, things give up
The tendency to fall. Things handled have,

Duchamp assures us, *the fatal tendency to secrete meaning.*

DROUGHT

Seeps of mineral stain

The rock face like tally marks.
A dry creek bed undercuts a wind-wrought cliff.

Polished to a dull luster,

The day moon is an exact facsimile of itself.
The spare haze of distant heat offers

A light reminiscent of rainfall

But when did the rain last fall and flood,
Gully-shed, then gone,

Slipped unseen through strata,

Through a warp and weft of stone,
To emerge again cleansed?

DEPARTURES

Galaxies I have not seen since childhood
Amass in the clear, dark desert sky.

::

Like the temporary configuration of a meander,
The original writing is effaced to make room for later writing.

::

The path switchbacks. How far down?
Cloud wisps on moss-edged crags.

::

Unmoved by white water: an ice-scoured boulder.
Beyond it: torn water repairs itself.

::

A language is lost, thus the knowledge it embodied.
A little boat is launched to set free a soul.

Acknowledgments

The author is grateful to the editors of the following journals, which first published many of these poems: *Allium, The Amsterdam Review, The Bennington Review, The Cimarron Review, Free State Review, Humana Obscura, Image, The Kenyon Review, Kestrel, Mudroom, The McNeese Review, Pensive, Superpresent, Terrain,* and *Valparaiso Poetry Review.*

The following poems are dedicated as follows:

"Confluence" for Jeff Hamilton
"Field Recording" for Jennifer Atkinson
"Desire Path" for Peter Streckfus
"Held Up to a Flame the Writing is Visible" for Steve Schreiner
"Evening Commotion" for H.L. Hix
"True Knowledge" for Allison Funk
"The Epic" for Jason Sommer
"Empty Calendar" for Sally Keith
"Stone City" for Jan Weissmiller
"Drought" for Arthur Sze
"Departures" for Charles Wright

Deep thanks to Martin Mitchell and Keene Carter for many rich and illuminating conversations about the art of poetry while many of these poems were being written.

Notes

The book's epigraph is from Wallace Stevens's "Of the Surface of Things" from 1919.

The poems in the book's final section are ekphrastic. The specific works and artists are detailed as follows:

"Empty Space Filled with Radio Waves" is in conversation with the paintings of Anselm Kiefer from his 2020 exhibition *Fur Walther Von Der Vogelweide* at the Thaddaeus Ropac Gallery in Salzburg, Austria.

"Lilith's Dream" is in conversation with Kiki Smith's sculpture "Lilith" at the Metropolitan Museum of Art in New York City.

"Afterbodings" is in conversation with the paintings of Kay Sage. Each of the eight subtitles is a title of one of her paintings. See *Kay Sage Catalogue Raisonné*, edited Jessie Sentivan, published by Delmonico-Prestel, 2018.

"Stone City" takes its title from and is in conversation with Grant Wood's "Stone City," which can be seen at the Joslyn Art Museum in Omaha, Nebraska.

"To Paint the Circumference of a Stone with a Feather" is in conversation with John Cage's "New River Watercolors Series," part of the 2012 exhibition, *John Cage at the Phillips*, at the Phillips Collection in Washington, DC.

"Relocation" is in conversation with the paintings of Gillian Lawler from her 2016 exhibition *Eminent Domain* at the Molesworth Gallery in Dublin, Ireland.

Notes

"Sacred Spaces" is in conversation with Callum Innes's painting "Exposed Painting Crimson Lake." Innes is represented by Sean Kelly Gallery, New York and Los Angeles.

"With Hidden Noise" takes its title from, and is in conversation with, the object "With Hidden Noise," by Marcel Duchamp, part of the 2019-2020 exhibition *Marcel Duchamp: The Barbara and Aaron Levine Collection* at the Hirshhorn Museum in Washington, DC.

"Drought" is in conversation with the contemplative space that is the Agnes Martin Gallery at the Harwood Museum of Art in Taos, New Mexico.

"Departures" is in conversation with the exhibition *Emmi Whitehorse: Mapping the Microcosm*, a 2019 exhibition at Chiaroscuro Contemporary Art in Santa Fe, New Mexico.

This book was set in Albertan, originally designed in 1982 as a metal-cut font by the distinguished Canadian type designer, Jim Rimmer, founder of Pie Tree Press. It was later digitized and released by Canada Type.

This book was designed by Shannon Carter, Ian Creeger, and Gregory Wolfe. It was published in hardcover, paperback, and electronic formats by Slant Books, Seattle, Washington.

Cover art: *Immigrant*, 2017, oil on canvas, 14 x 18 inches. Courtesy John Dilg and Galerie Eva Presenhuber, Zurich/Vienna. © John Dilg.

www.ingramcontent.com/pod-product-compliance
Lightning Source LLC
Chambersburg PA
CBHW032242080426
42735CB00008B/959